ZACK C. WOOTEN

Unauthorized Biography of MrBeast

The Untold Story of Jimmy Donaldson, the YouTube Phenom who is Using His Platform to Make a Difference in the World

Copyright © 2023 by Zack C. Wooten

All rights reserved. No part of this publication may be reproduced, stored or transmitted in any form or by any means, electronic, mechanical, photocopying, recording, scanning, or otherwise without written permission from the publisher. It is illegal to copy this book, post it to a website, or distribute it by any other means without permission.

First edition

This book was professionally typeset on Reedsy.
Find out more at reedsy.com

Contents

Early Life	1
Who is Jimmy Donaldson	1
Family Background	1
Educational Background	6
Net worth	7
Relationship	8
Marital Relationship	8
Who is the ex-girlfriend of Mr. Beast?	8
Fast Facts About Thea Booysen, Mr. Beast's Girlfriend	10
Thea Booysen and Mr. Beast's Relationship	11
Was It Truly the Case That Mr. Beast Tested His Girlfriend?	11
The Effect on Mr. Beast's Career of His Girlfriend	12
The Difficulties of Reaching Out to YouTube Influencers	12
Friendship-based relationship	13
Major Accomplishment	15
His Aim	20
Struggles and Challenges	27
Career Difficulties	27
Health Challenge	28
The security issue he encountered	28
Legacy and Impact	30
A Few Notable Achievements	30
Legacy and Impact	30
Things to learn from MrBeast	33

Early Life

Who is Jimmy Donaldson

In real life, his name is Jimmy Donaldson, MrBeast is the stage name.
Work as a YouTuber; born in Wichita, Kansas, USA;
Date of birth: May 7, 1998,
Age :25
Gender : Male
Nationality: American
Marriage Status: Single
Name of the school he attend: Greenville Christian Academy .

Family Background

Donaldson claims that he has no memories of his childhood until the age of eleven.

He owes part of this to his business acumen. He boasts, "I'm very forward-thinking."Ignore what happened in the past. It has already occurred. My ambition is to conquer the future.
In reality, it seems that he was born without the nostalgia gene: despite having one, he has never visited his mother's vast warehouse, where she stores all of the memorabilia from his past films.

Given the turbulent circumstances of his upbringing, Donaldson's lack of nostalgia might be a defense strategy. He was born in Kansas, the middle child of two active-duty military members. Sue, his mother, was a prison warden in Mannheim before transferring to Fort Leavenworth.

"Jammy finds it pretty impressive that his mother managed a prison," Sue, a reticent woman with a reasonably long carrot-colored haircut, says.

She is now the top compliance officer of MrBeast LLC, overseeing the company's spending and contracts as well as her son's personal affairs, including his banking. (She even picked the house where he lives.)

Sue worked 12-hour days while on active service, and a rotating set of au pairs took care of the children. She claims that Jimmy is introverted since they moved around a much.

"We lived in three different locations in the southern U.S." before he was seven years old, she continues. "There were no aunts, uncles, or cousins in attendance." It was really just the two of us.

Donaldson's parents separated in 2007 when he was eight years old, ending a difficult marriage, and he hasn't talked to his father since. He declined to elaborate on the reasons why in public.

Sue views her divorce as something she "just tried my hardest to keep everything moving forward as best as possible." "We managed to get through it as best we could."

Donaldson had few friends as a child and didn't spend much time with other kids on weekends. Sue immediately recognized his competitive nature. "It was hard to have fun with him.

"Everything was always required to play through everything," she alleges. Comparable to Monopoly. We eventually wanted to throw it out since he was behaving as if he was giving us Boardwalk and Park.

"Anybody who had previously known Jimmy would say, 'Really?'" Is Jimmy well-known? He was completely quiet the whole time.

Even people who know Donaldson are surprised by his choice to live in front of the camera. "Anyone who knew Jimmy before would say, 'Really?'""How did Jimmy become famous?" Tyson, his close friend, wonders.

He was completely quiet the whole time. But it's not like he shunned social encounters. Jimmy just likes chatting about his hobbies, which are mostly video games and YouTube. He will not speak if no one else is discussing such subjects.

Those who know Donaldson well simply use the word "obsessive" to describe him; he has a tendency to fixate on one issue at the expense of all others. He believes that due of his excessive YouTube viewing, people at his school began labeling him as autistic.

"There was a period of five years in my life when I was utterly, unhealthy fixated on researching virality and the YouTube algorithm," he said. "I arrived. I'd use Uber Eats to order food.
  Then I'd spend the rest of the day on my computer studying bullshit with [other YouTubers]. Furthermore, during a time featuring Settlers of Catan, Donaldson's assistant purchased five copies of the strategy game every month to guarantee that there were always "new ones" available.
  "I'm great at lying," Donaldson deadpans, appreciating the tactics and machinations required.

Donaldson seemed to be an unusual choice to be the face of a multibillion-dollar media conglomerate. As an introvert, he often expresses his discomfort with casual interaction.
  On our first encounter, he approached me in the driveway of his sprawling 60,000-square-foot studio and said, "So, we're going to start talking now?"

Naturally, this kind of donation is analogous to bandaging a brain tumor. It may be eye-catching, but it ignores cyclical poverty and persistent structural inequities.

Over lunch at a Mexican restaurant, I remark to Donaldson and the two boys, Jacobs and Tareq Salameh (a former wannabe comic turned cameraman who was promoted to the cast) that all of their videos appear to be based on the idea that a big check or a wad of cash stuffed in a fist can heal all kinds of ailments.

But, owing to his ever-more-extreme actions, he eventually gained admirers and scraped by. Tyson wraps him in 100 layers of Saran wrap and ilet paper in one video; in another, Donaldson counts to 100,000, a notion he says he got from hoping to earn money by viewing numerous Naruto anime episodes in one sitting.

"I hope you have at least 100k subs," he stated in a 2015 video for a future version of himself. In May of 2017, he would have one million subscribers.

Sue was surprised to hear that he was making YouTube videos from a note in his yearbook, since she had no idea. As she describes it, "I was a normal parent." "What was out there worried me a great deal."

Her concern was alleviated when Donaldson revealed that he was prospering from his channel. Nonetheless, Mom urged that Jimmy attend college and graduate with a degree.

Donaldson eventually succumbed and enrolled at a community college, but he says he did not attend any courses and dropped out in the midst of the first semester.

Sue did this when her son was evicted from the house and moved into a duplex with Tyson. Donaldson had just hit 750,000 subscribers and signed his first brand contract, so the timing couldn't have been better.

Instead of squandering it, he used it to produce a film in which he delivers a $10,000 check to a homeless person.

Although this was not Donaldson's first video in which he gave out money for free, he could see that people identified with this kind of faked charity.

He rapidly found himself generating $100,000 per month from his channel after moving to videos that were more giveaway-focused, such as "Tipping Waitresses With Real Gold Bars" (53 million views).

She says, "He came in one day with a check and was like, 'Mom, look how much I just made.'" "And that was my salary for the entire year." She began working for the firm shortly after retirement.

Donaldson says he doesn't care about money and plans to give it all before dying. While driving around in his Tesla Model X, he says, "I don't want to live my life chasing the next shiny object to the next shiny object." "It's a depressing and miserable way to live."

His Parents

Mr. Beast's parents are Mr. and Mrs. Stephen Donaldson. His father is a businessman, while his mother is a well-known homemaker. Jimmy has a strong relationship with his mother, whom he once surprised with a $10,000 cash surprise and a home makeover.

His relationship with his Mother

Mr. Beast is close to his mother, who has appeared in a handful of his films. She's also featured in a number of his prank films.

Sisters and Brothers

MrBeast has just one sibling, Charles "CJ" Donaldson. He, like his younger brother, is interested in making content, albeit he is not as well-known.

Educational Background

Educational Background

Donaldson went to a tiny, private school called Greenville Christian Academy, where male pupils had to compose Bible verses as a form of discipline in addition to being penalized for having long hair.

Because "you have it beat into your head every day," he claims he was reared as an observant person. However, he eventually began to have reservations about the church's beliefs on matters such as homosexuality and changed his identity to an agnostic.

"So many people around here find this to be such a sensitive topic," he says. "While I do believe in God, there are a lot of different faiths and a lot of individuals who have strong religious beliefs. Selecting the correct [religion] is a challenging task.

After graduating from Greenville Christian Academy, Mr. Beast left college early in 2016 to focus on his full-time YouTube career. His older brother, CJ Donaldson, is the owner of the YouTube channel titled

His house

Because of his enormous wealth, people are always enthralled by the appearance of Mr. Beast's house. Another story goes that a rich guy lives in an extravagant home during his free time.

It's interesting that the YouTuber is difficult to find since he has properties in many US states. For example, he is said to own residences in Georgia, Los Angeles, and Kansas.

Given how eager he is to find new places for his movies, it should come as no surprise that he owns many dwellings.

His Car

In addition to his YouTube channel, MrBeast stands out for his passion for fast automobiles and the fact that he really owns one. Among his many amazing cars are a Lamborghini Huracan Spyder, Tesla Model 3, BMW i8, Dodge Grand Caravan, Mercedes G63 AMG, and more.

Net worth

One of the richest video makers on YouTube, Instagram, and other platforms is MrBeast. However, his most famous platform is YouTube, where his films have brought him a sizable income.

Approximations of Mr. Beast's fortune vary between the sources. But according to Forbes, he is estimated to be worth a whopping $500 million.

Relationship

Marital Relationship

Who is the ex-girlfriend of Mr. Beast?

The ex-girlfriend of Mr. Beast is Maddy Spidell. In June of 2019, they went on a date. Their relationship ended in 2022, after they had first connected on Twitter.

Maddy Spidell is a popular figure on social media, especially on TikTok and Instagram, where she has a sizable fan base. She has been showing off her dancing skills on social media for years. She is also a skilled dancer.

Maddy and MrBeast, whose true name is Jimmy Donaldson, got together on Twitter in 2019 and started dating.
    Before announcing their split to the world in early 2022, they had been together for around three years. A lot of their fans expressed regret when they announced their breakup, which sparked a lot of activity on social media.

Jimmy and Maddy ended their prior relationship, but they have stayed in great contact and have nothing but wonderful things to say about it. They run their own social media sites and provide their fans with updates on their life.

RELATIONSHIP

Jimmy Donaldson, the well-known Mr. Beast, is no longer with his ex-girlfriend Maddy Spidell. A few months ago, the internet went berserk when they announced that their one-year romance was ending.

In addition, the statement claims that Maddy and Mr. Beast dated for three years before calling it quits.

She made her feature film debut in Surprising My Girlfriend With 100,000 Roses for Valentine's Day. She also had two brief cameos in the movies, I Spent 50 Hours In Solitary Confinement and I Adopted EVERY Dog In A Dog Shelter.

She is sometimes discussed on the MrBeast channels, despite the fact that she seldom appears there.

Thea Booysen is Mr. Beast's current girlfriend, and they just began dating. Currently, their connection is built on distance since she resides in South Africa. Though their relationship is by no means simple, they get along pretty well and see one other as much as they should.

In addition to being the author of "The Marked Children," Booysen writes about esports and creates content. According to reports, they started dating in February 2022.

In an episode of the podcast "Wide Awake" the following October, Booysen revealed their relationship to the public.

On social media, the pair has openly acknowledged one another, but they haven't disclosed many personal information about their union.

Mr. Beast seems content with Thea Booysen's relationship, in contrast to his previous one.

He shared a lovely photo of them on vacation in the Maldives on his Instagram story to show off their love.

Fans anxiously anticipated news of their relationship after seeing their cute photos of the couple vacationing in the Maldives.

Mr. Beast has officially ended all rumors and conjecture over his love status with this declaration.

Thea is mostly recognized on the Twitch streaming network, in contrast to her boyfriend. By airing games like the very popular Gwent and The Witcher, Thea has amassed a fan base of over 27,000. Similar videos are also posted by her on her YouTube account.

The 25-year-old, who is South African by birth, has had a long and successful online career.

When Mr. Beast and a few other well-known designers visited South Africa, Thea got to know him. She was curious to see him because she wanted to know who was really behind the generosity and viral pranks.

She and Jimmy got along well when they got together for coffee. Ever since the latter part of 2022, they have continued to be connected.

Fast Facts About Thea Booysen, Mr. Beast's Girlfriend

With her virtual profession and moniker Mr Beast GF, Thea has an unusual existence away from the spotlight.

She has degrees in both law and psychology. She is now enrolled at the University of Edinburgh to pursue a master's degree in neuropsychology.

Thea has also produced written works. "The Marked Children," her young adult novel, was published in August 2022. The book is now rated 4.6 stars on Amazon, where it is regarded as a "exciting sci-fi novel."

Due to her intense passion for "The Witcher," the well-known Mr. Beast enthusiast has been appointed as the official ESports presenter for the Polish video game studio CDPR. She has been spotted directing a number of the game's and its sequels'-related events.

Thea Booysen and Mr. Beast's Relationship

The majority of details surrounding Mr. Beast and his fiancée's relationship are unknown. They make an effort to maintain their personal lives apart from their online personas since they are often in the spotlight.

On social media, however, it seems that the two enjoying hanging around and have posted a ton of pictures. After dating for more than a year, the pair seems content and prosperous in their relationship.

Was It Truly the Case That Mr. Beast Tested His Girlfriend?

The well-known Mr. Beast fan said in a podcast from October 2022 that she had been unintentionally put to the test when they first started dating.

Thea confided in Jimmy during their coffee meeting that she felt comfortable answering his inquiries. But as time passed, she learned that the donor was really screening potential matches with a pre-made list of questions!
 Mr. Beast has also said that he was compelled to take this little test because, as a well-known internet personality, he has sometimes wondered why individuals do the things that they do.

Fortunately for him, Thea turned out to be the genuine thing, and their accidental encounter blossomed into a wonderful partnership!

The Effect on Mr. Beast's Career of His Girlfriend

Most of MrBeast's fans support his new partner, particularly after hearing about him on a previous podcast.

Jimmy had the most amazing responses when asked how Thea has affected his life! He emphasized how important she is to him and how she eases his tension and allows him to unwind.

Additionally, he expressed how significant it was to him since the Twitch broadcaster is a familiar face and constant source of support.

The Difficulties of Reaching Out to YouTube Influencers

Even if Ms Beast's new partner hasn't released an official statement, it's clear that she benefits from their connection. For instance, since their relationship started, her Twitch following has probably grown significantly, giving her access to new chances.

However, Maddy, Mr. Beast's ex-girlfriend, has expressed her displeasure on social media about receiving hate mail from Mr. Beast's followers after their split.
    She said that she received criticism even though she had done nothing wrong in her prior relationship with Jimmy.

Thea Booysen, sometimes referred to as TheaBeasty, is a well-known social media figure who is most recognized for her Twitch gaming broadcasts in which she engages with fans while engaging in popular games.
    The twenty-five-year-old studies neuropsychology at the University of Edinburgh and is a published author.

Thea and MrBeast started dating near the close of 2022. Together, they have appeared in a number of live and virtual events.

Taking everything into account, we're happy to see Jimmy back in the dating game and hope that his celebrity won't interfere with his goal for a happy, regular existence.

He started his YouTube channel and has grown to be one of the most popular accounts on the network over time.

Because of the popularity of his films, he wanted to learn more about the gaming community and started a new channel.

Friendship-based relationship

Donaldson acknowledges that he has found it challenging to form personal ties because of his intense concentration on his career. To quote him directly, "I'm not really good at keeping friends."

"Work is the center of all my friends' lives." Not only that, but he doesn't spend much time with his family—his elder brother, who lives nearby and is referred to by another YouTuber as "less successful" than he is. Donaldson laments that his brother's channel is now referred to as "MrBro," saying this is unfortunate.

Actually, at the age of eleven, Donaldson became well-known on the internet by posting videos of himself playing games like Call of Duty and Minecraft.

With the moniker "Mr. Beast" already taken, the 13-year-old created a second channel under the identity "MrBeast6000."

Initially, it seemed as if Donaldson was experimenting with various YouTube trends to see what would catch on in an attempt to find out who he was: After attempting to commentate on video games in the vein of PewDiePie, he proceeded to create videos where he estimated the earnings of other

YouTubers.

Major Accomplishment

Jimmy Donaldson is a 25-year-old philanthropist who goes by the internet moniker MrBeast.

MrBeast, a Kansas native, made his internet debut in 2012. He has over 150 million YouTube followers and is now the fourth most subscribed channel during the last 11 years.

Nevertheless, in February 2012, at the age of 13, he posted his first video to YouTube under the alias "MrBeast6000."

MrBeast made films that he believed would appeal to the largest audience in an attempt to dominate the YouTube algorithm for the first several years, but his efforts were in vain.

"If it gets the most views, its because people click on it and I want to give them what they want," MrBeast said.

With his hilarious compilations of his best moments from games like "Minecraft" and "Call of Duty," his evaluations of YouTuber wealth, his guidance for aspiring content creators, and his commentary on drama involving other creators, MrBeast tried to manipulate YouTube's algorithm, and his popularity fluctuated over time.

MrBeast was absent from a large number of his early films.

MrBeast's "worst intros" series of videos, which gathered and parodied YouTuber beginnings he encountered on the network, helped him become well-known in 2015 and 2016. MrBeast had thirty thousand clients by the middle of 2016.

Despite the fact that MrBeast joined in college throughout the end of 2016, it's challenging to locate any information regarding him.

The YouTuber claimed to have dropped out of college after only two weeks, telling his mother, "I'd rather be poor than do anything except YouTube."

His mother forced MrBeast to leave his boyhood home in North Carolina when he turned eighteen, "because she loves me and just wants me to be successful," he tweeted in November of that year.

MrBeast posted a video of himself counting to 100,000 in January 2017, and it went viral very fast. He then said that he needed forty-four hours to complete the film.

Mr. Beast said, "I just really wanted it," as soon as he accepted the assignment. "I knew it would go viral. I dropped out of college because I wasn't making much money."

MrBeast discovered what the YouTube algorithm likes after the first video got popular. Similar efforts, such as spinning a fidget spinner for a whole day and playing Jake Paul's "Its Everyday Bro" music video nonstop for ten hours, rapidly brought him additional views. MrBeast has one million members as of November 2017.

These days, the majority of the videos on MrBeast's channel are of a few different kinds. He continues to pull lengthy, tiresome practical jokes that have earned him the nickname "junklord YouTube," such as last-minute contests where he awards thousands of dollars.

Two of these films are "Last To Remove Hand, Gets Lamborghini Challenge" and "Going Through the Same Drive Thru 1,000 Times".

Mr. Beast also does amazing acts for donations and charity. In addition, he started a vehicle firm and offered free automobiles to everyone.

He allegedly provided small-time Twitch and YouTube broadcasters, restaurants, and Uber drivers thousands of dollars.

Thanks to the growth of his YouTube channel, MrBeast has been able to recruit four of his boyhood friends: Chandler, Garret, Jake, and Chris. The gang has gained popularity inside the MrBeast empire and often appears in the most ridiculous last-person-to-leave contests.

With his outrageous deeds, MrBeast raised $1 million by December 2018, making him the "Biggest Philanthropist on YouTube." It was his own viral material that made MrBeast famous; he can only part with these thousands of dollars because he has six-figure sponsor agreements funding in-video advertising.

MrBeast is well-known for having contributed to the emergence of a brand-new subgenre of pricey stunt movies on YouTube, whereby directors do intricate tasks and lavishly fund prizes.

In 2012, he registered on YouTube and began uploading videos. His YouTube video series, Worst Intros, helped him become well-known.

His fame grew when he began sharing videos of himself playing computer games, such Factions: Minecraft. A Guy Buried Round 50 Black Ops 2 Zombies and Sent His Home in Our Base.

After a few years of uploading videos on YouTube about video games, he started making pricey videos that required a sizable sum of money.

Actually, Mr. Beast began spending thousands of dollars on the internet, creating original films like $5 For Hot Girls To Advertise Your YouTube Channel.

Mr. Beast became well-known around the country when he began sharing emotional films on the internet, such "Giving $10,000 to a Random Homeless Man." He kept making movies of this kind, saying that the money he was giving away came from an app called "Quidd."

He then began making random financial donations to Twitch broadcasters. Mr. Beast didn't stop there, even though his channel had millions of subscribers at this point. He continued to make movies that no one else had seen or heard of.

I Flew Using Only Leaf Blowers, I Donated $30,000 To A Random Twitch Streamer, I Bought A Car Using Only Pennies, and Can 100,000 Pieces Of Paper Stop A Bullet? are some of the most popular videos on his channel.

In addition, he oversees several additional YouTube channels. Beast Philanthropy, MrBeast Gaming, Beast Reacts, and MrBeast Shorts are a few of them.

On other social networking sites, Mr. Beast has a lot of popularity. He sells T-shirts and other apparel items on his internet shop. Mr. Beast works for a business named "Quidd."

Donaldson portrays the lead role on his MrBeast YouTube channel. With sophisticated, well-produced films that have vibrant thumbnails that cost $10,000 each to develop, he draws in 93.9 million viewers.
Videos with titles like "Extreme $1,000,000 Hide-and-Seek" and "World's Most Dangerous Escape Room" are intentionally made to play well on YouTube's algorithm.

There are bins full of inflatable dinosaur costumes for a movie called "Walking Into Random Stores With 100 Dinosaurs" and mounds of GameStop merchandise from a video where he pledged to purchase anything a contestant could put within a circle ("He just wanted cash instead," Donaldson adds).
A photo of one billion Orbeez, which are small gel-filled pellets, may be found in the rear. In 2018, Donaldson staged a movie in his closest friend's backyard.

Using his reputation for pulling off incredible pranks, MrBeast helped

MAJOR ACCOMPLISHMENT

PewDiePie, a well-known YouTuber who was vying to become the channel with the most subscribers in late 2018 (a title he has since lost to T-Series).

He went all out and produced a 12-hour tape in which he repeatedly said the term "PewDiePie" 100,000 times, in typical MrBeast way. Moreover, he showed up at the Super Bowl wearing shirts that said "Sub 2 PewDiePie."

MrBeast started the TeamTrees fundraising initiative in October with the goal of planting 20 million trees by the end of 2019.

Over 600 influencers have endorsed the project, and internet moguls like Elon Musk, Sidepiece, Jeffree Star on YouTube, and Twitter CEO Jack Dorsey have contributed up to $18 million thus far.

MrBeast shares a diverse array of stuff on his channels, including expensive practical jokes, footage of incredible survival, and charitable content.

In addition, he sells Karl Gummies, milk chocolate bars, and hamburgers under his own brand! You could count on one hand the things he hasn't done at this point.

His Aim

Prior to working for Donaldson, the biggest celebrity on YouTube, had lawn chairs in his living room and mattresses on the floor, according to his assistant, a model-handsome transplant from Utah called Steele. Donaldson's ex-girlfriend had also just renovated his kitchen.

Trumpson says, "I don't give a shit about looks." "My only concern is functionality."

It is also possible that he is obsessed with the expense of some bright goods, as seen by the $50,000 he spent installing his specially designed double-sided refrigerator, which he bought so his chef could take food inside without bothering him.

Essentially, it seems that Donaldson sees money as a weapon to help him reach his dominance objective within the YouTube community.

He responds, "It doesn't matter to me," in reference to the heaps of cash, Lamborghinis, and gold bars in his warehouse.

To others, however, it matters. And that's what enables us to get views, which enables me to accept larger assignments and be paid more.

The amount of money Donaldson spends on his movies has increased along with his subscription base. The most of them these days need around a million dollars to develop, and very few of them turn a profit.

Donaldson's "gaming" and "reacts" channels, which are very profitable and feature the boys prominently, contribute significantly to the main channel's earnings.

"I could be making videos for less money," declares Donaldson. But I'm simply not interested in. My goal is to exceed expectations and achieve more success.

After spending more than $4 million to recreate the Netflix series Squid Game albeit without the gory violence and awarding the winner with a $456,000 reward during a stressful game of musical chairs, Donaldson's amazing ability to hack YouTube garnered international attention in late 2021. Over 225 million people watched the video after it became viral.

"I aim to become the most popular YouTube channel ever." Not for my own ego, either. It only gives me a goal to work for and a reason to get out of bed. Vanity, yet, is also what it is.

But for many others, the Squid Game remake was a misappropriation of the original series' content, which illustrated the terrible consequences of unfettered capitalism on middle-class living.

Donaldson brushes the criticism aside. He says, "I like how these people are acting out the show." The creator of the program said just that."

The creator of Squid Game, Hwang Dong-Hyuk, did express his approval of YouTubers copying the series; he only made no mention of Mr. Beast's video in particular.

Donaldson has previously been involved in controversy. Using homophobic obscenities in his adolescent tweets, he made fun of homosexuality in several of his films, The Atlantic found in 2018.

In instead of apologising, he told the magazine at the time, "I'm not offensive in the slightest in anything I do." I'm just going to choose to ignore it. It doesn't appear like anybody is concerned about this. Today he regrets it even more.

"This is literally the heart of the Bible Belt," he tells me as we enter Greenville by vehicle. When I was younger, my morning thought would be, "God is going to burn this Earth because of gay people."

He used to say that this made comments that were disparaging of LGBT persons "normal." I became aware that this was unusual as I got older.

I was merely reared in a peculiar environment. Consequently, I [wish I could] go back in time and tell them to cease behaving that way.

Donaldson's group includes a few other people who have also come under fire for their remarks on social media. Tyson is one such individual who, in April 2021, came under fire for posting memes that were homophobic and transphobic.

Tyson said he was sorry, removed the offending tweets, and described the incident as "an opportunity for learning and growth." He claimed that his own issues with his sexuality were the reason for the tweets, having come out as bisexual in the autumn of 2020.

Donaldson joked that he sexually identifies as an assault helicopter and a tank in a 2016 video that went viral the previous year. It seemed as if he was making fun of transvestism.

The video was developed in response to a joke that first appeared on Reddit and 4chan. In the video that was subsequently removed, he asks, "Is someone just sitting there and getting paid to think of genders?"

The transphobic joke was rather popular at the time, but Donaldson says he has no idea where it originated. He describes the video as "jokes" and claims, "I was just following along with everyone else who was doing the meme."

Because of his strong dedication to being politically impartial, at least in public, Donaldson has avoided criticism. He continues, "I don't want to alienate Democrats and Republicans."

That anyone may help my charitable endeavors is excellent. Feeding hundreds of millions of people is my objective. Therefore, if I insulted over half of American culture, I would be foolish.

He was most recently on Joe Rogan's podcast, which has been under fire for spreading misinformation about vaccines and Covid denial even though these subjects were not discussed on the show.

With statements from multiple former employees accusing Donaldson of creating a hostile work environment, yelling at employees, forcing them to put in excessive hours, and using derogatory language, the New York Times' 2021 investigation posed perhaps the biggest threat to MrBeast's reputation as a family-friendly company.

Due to the hate they were experiencing from MrBeast supporters, Nate Anderson and Matt Turner, two of the former MrBeast editors who came out against him, erased the videos they had created about their experiences.

The assertions stated in the Times article are disputed by Donaldson. I have, in fact, collaborated with more than a thousand individuals. He continues by saying, "It was acceptable that two people thought I was extremely demanding."

Despite our stringent rules, our workplace is safe. Turner claims that after his dismissal, he offered him $10,000 and put him forward for a job at a gaming firm. But according to Turner, the real sum his pay to the conclusion of his contract was less.

Tyson points out that Donaldson has trouble communicating, which contributes to the issues at work.

According to him, "I think he also has a very hard time socializing, even though he knows what he wants." I believe he struggles to express his needs and desires to others, even though we've spoken about it.

Turner, however, was affected profoundly by those awkward meetings: "You see him on camera and you're like, 'He's such a cool dude.'" "Damn, I wish the cool Jimmy was the real Jimmy," you would remark if you knew him.

Teflon is certainly made more appealing by Donaldson's increasing prominence as a philanthropist.

He used to specialize on visually amazing YouTube pranks, but in recent years, he has started making more humanitarian films.

In addition to starting MrBeast Philanthropy, whose CEO, Darren Margolias, oversees the weekly food and clothing donations made possible by YouTuber merchandise, Donaldson also rose to prominence with the Arbor Day Foundation by starting TeamSeas and TeamTrees.

While there is debate about whether planting 20 million trees would have an environmental effect, Dan Lambe, CEO of the Arbor Day Foundation, believes TeamTrees delivers a powerful statement despite accusations from corporate funders that these initiatives are just greenwashing. As he puts it, "planting 20 million trees is not going to solve the climate crisis."

On the other hand, it is beneficial to stress the need and advantages of planting trees. With 14 million trees planted thus far, Lambe believes TeamTrees is on pace to reach its target by the end of the year.

Donaldson was not exposed to charitable giving throughout his formative years. Sue claims he has never given his religion to volunteerism or community service, and he denies having a strong emotional connection with any of the issues he supports.

Nonetheless, Margolias claims that Donaldson's early experiences of donating money to the homeless via brand partnerships "lit a fire" inside of him and motivated him to use his influence and ability to improve the world.

By supporting a range of humanitarian endeavors, Margolias claims that Donaldson aspires to teach an a new generation about the advantages of selfless giving. Although he acknowledges that the majority of his viewership is under twelve, YouTube statistics do not keep track of people under that age.

Donaldson wants to become the most successful YouTuber of all time, get 100 million followers, and expand Mr. Beast Burger locations; he is more focused on building his business than dating.

He is more focused on expanding his impact on the platform that originally made him famous than he is on landing a big music contract or a Netflix deal, in contrast to many other entrepreneurs who go to the mainstream entertainment industry for validation.

It is strange that Donaldson, who is completely enthralled with the platform, claims not to watch YouTube videos on a regular basis anymore. Rather, he's become intensely obsessed with the concept of self-improvement.

As a motivating technique, he put up a gym in the center of his kitchen so that he would work out rather than grab a snack. He just finished reading a biography of Michael Jordan.

He often reads biographies of very successful persons. Additionally, he engaged a life coach and discovered that successful men reach their prime around the age of 40.

He responds, "At first, I thought you were fucking crazy." But, I suppose, I believe it. Therefore, as long as your body is in good health, wrinkles won't form. Moreover, if you're wealthy and own additional comparable belongings.

He will not tolerate any hindrances in his way, and if his life coach is correct, he has almost ten years to reach his peak. In order to work from anywhere in the MrBeast LLC studio, he claims he will put a shower in his office once the renovations are finished.

He said, "I just need to grind, be obsessed, and never give up." "don't want to let your exponential growth curve flatline if it is."

Because of this mindset, his YouTube channel is now the fifth most popular in the world. Of course, he wants to be the first.

That's why there are genuine sharks, lime-green Lambos, odd settings, more elaborate stunts, million dollar bills, and tens of millions more in the bank; even if it doesn't seem like enough.

That's "this is really all I do," he replies from the driver's seat of his Tesla. "I stay away from social events. I wouldn't say we're pals. I also run the danger of thinking to myself when I'm fifty, "Damn, I really only did that one thing and nothing else."

Struggles and Challenges

Career Difficulties

A YouTuber named FlyyDoesYT accused Mr. Beast of altering his videos in 2018. Following FlyyDoesYT's week-long tenure as Mr. Beast's editor, a lot of people viewed the 25-minute video which was rife with accusations with extreme caution.

However, not everyone has accepted Mr. Beast's notoriety without reservation. The Atlantic discovered several other, since-deleted tweets from Mr. Beast from 2018, in which he makes fun of homosexuality and uses homophobic epithets.

He tweeted, "Just because I'm gay doesn't mean I'm gai," at the time the story was published. In self-defense, Mr. Beast said, "Not in the slightest bit offensive in anything I do."

Additionally, MrBeast was accused of disbursing counterfeit money when it was discovered via criticism that the notes used in a November 2019 film were not real money.

Mr. Beast then revealed that he had given fictitious checks to the individuals in the video in order to reduce the possibility of an irrational crowd swarming for free money.

Mr. Beast was accused by another YouTuber of mistreating his staff members by having them record one of his films for an uploaded video. Moreover, he has said that Mr. Beast is not really himself when he is in front of the camera.

Mr. Beast said he wasn't performing for the camera and that, in response to the charges, he had really made a sizable financial donation.

He advised "FlyyDoesYT" or anybody else to approach the money receivers and inquire as to whether they had indeed received the funds.

Moreover, he refuted any allegations of mistreating his staff, claiming to have Crohn's illness and to have requested them to finish the films when he wasn't feeling well.

Health Challenge

MrBeast has divulged a few personal information about himself throughout the years. Claiming to suffer from Crohn's disease, a chronic inflammatory bowel illness, is the 25-year-old.

Even though he had always loved baseball, Donaldson gave up sports in his sophomore year of high school after learning he had Crohn's disease, an inflammatory condition marked by stomach pain.

Although he often has flare-ups, Remicade is now being utilized to treat his symptoms. Moreover, he employs a personal chef to prepare his meals.

Sue claims that Donaldson's decision to use YouTube was prompted by his increased inside time as a result of the stress of managing his Crohn's disease.

The security issue he encountered

There are security worries because of his well-known wealth. After his flat was broken into during a film shoot three or four years ago, he moved into a gated neighborhood and into a home with triple-steel reinforced doors and bulletproof glass.

Every time he ventures out in public in Greenville, a bodyguard follows him. These worries don't appear to be unwarranted: Before we leave the Mexican restaurant, we wait outside in the parking lot for hours, and two young people start to follow Donaldson's vehicle.

Donaldson admits that he is the root of the issue. He said, "I can make any world I want, create any content I want, and I choose this." "I have a great deal of power [in the end]. I had enough of money if I wanted it. Boo hooray, I'm the one being looked forward to. I'll succeed.

Legacy and Impact

A Few Notable Achievements

- His Streamy Award has been won.
- He is declared the "Breakout Creator" prize winner.2021
- He Discovers the Game "Finger on the App": This thrilling game pays $25k to the final player remaining.
- Child of the Year Award nominee
- He is a nominee for the title of "Best Male Social Star."

Legacy and Impact

Donaldson says he often receives messages from parents telling him how seeing his films inspired their kids to help out at a soup kitchen or clean up rubbish on the beach.

I spoke with a lot of parents of Mr. Beast fans, and many of them indicated that their kids forced them to give to TeamTrees or TeamSeas.

However, it hits home when I suggest that the Mr. Beast films can present a cynical image of generosity. Donaldson responds, "Your worry isn't even a concern whatsoever."

Millions of children these days are not documenting their incredible achievements. In other words, millions of children are doing well.

Donaldson built a multi-media empire with the boys at his side that generated an estimated $54 million in revenue for his primary channel last year.

Furthermore, he has 1,600 franchises for his delivery-only restaurant, MrBeast Burger, which is modeled like a ghost kitchen.

He debuted a brand of chocolate bars in January called Feastables, and the advertising campaign was dubbed "Win Mr. Beast's Chocolate Factory," alluding to Willy Wonka. Sales are thought to bring in around half a million dollars a month for him.

In less than ten years, Donaldson moved from creating DVDs with commentary on video games in his bedroom to overseeing sixty full-time workers, excluding independent contractors.

He is the creator of several well-known charitable initiatives, such as TeamSeas, which seeks to remove 30 million pounds of garbage from the ocean, and TeamTrees, which seeks to plant 20 million trees worldwide after receiving $20 million in contributions.

Greenville, North Carolina, the hometown of Donaldson, is now seeing the construction of three massive content and production centers by his firm.

little city of Greenville is home to strip malls, office parks, and the campus of East Carolina University. Donaldson wants to establish Greenville as a center for people who produce material for digital media.

Margolias is an early-forties guy who is substantial and serious. "So many people are conditioned to think giving money to charity is a burden or a sacrifice," he says. "But people's perceptions of giving will shift when they realize that helping others is lovely and enjoyable."

Margolias claims that Donaldson's charitable activities are largely hidden from public view.

He cites several instances in which he donated tens of thousands of dollars to buy Christmas gifts for children whose families perished in hurricanes or to rent and furnish a home for a family of nine whose parents were laid off as a result of the pandemic.

Jimmy told me the night we met that his goal in life is to make the world a better place. He declares, "There's no denying that's genuine.

To those who remark, "He does it for the views," let me to clarify that we have accomplished some really lovely things, all of which Jimmy pays for entirely with his own funds and of which no one is aware.

Questions about Donaldson's intentions are addressed tactfully.

"I have nothing to prove to anyone, and I am confident in who I am."

He states, "I think my accomplishments speak for themselves." "I have invested an unreasonable amount of time and energy into creating a channel for my charity, but I will never get any income from it.

Every month, I waste hundreds of hours and five figures. Millions of dollars' worth of chances might be awarded to initiatives. because I don't give a damn. I don't say these things in public because I don't do these things for that reason.

Things to learn from MrBeast

This world's most famous YouTuber continues to grow in popularity because to his larger-than-life exploits and extravagant gifts. He pushes the limits of what is possible and seems to have a genius level awareness of what works on YouTube.

While not all, if any, content producers want to create the kind of material that MrBeast does, what content creator wouldn't want to imitate his success in their own niche?

With that in mind, MrBeast's proven content development experience has yielded 11 advice for prospective producers.

1. FIND YOUR PASSION, SAYS MRBEAST.
You may not be MrBeast (although if you are, hello MrBeast, nice to see you again), but you can be the MrBeast of your field. It all begins with discovering your passion and pursuing it wholeheartedly.

MrBeast built his own luck by determining what he was passionate about and then pursuing it. So go ahead and do it.

2. MAKE GOOD FRIENDS, SAYS MRBEAST.
Seek for chances to team up. Creating content can be isolating. Find individuals with whom you wish to collaborate in order to learn, share, brainstorm, and encourage one another.

Give and receive constructive criticism that is both honest and constructive. Sincere criticism from other artists may help you better your work.

Content producers may learn from one other's errors and accomplishments by forming a small but close network.

3. MRBEAST SAYS: CONSIDER VIRAL

MrBeast obviously knows that virality does not happen by chance. However, "going viral" does not have to imply inventing the next dance fad or flooding a garden with 100 million Orbeez. Consider what virality implies in relation to your niche.

Make fascinating content that people will want to watch and share. Consider what you can do to attract attention in your niche. MrBeast believes that "I like bananas" is insufficient.

"Bananas are the best food on the planet," as the saying goes. Fruit is probably not your content specialty (or are bananas berries?), so consider how this tip applies to your content and be brave.

4. RE-INVEST, SAYS MRBEAST

MrBeast invests much on his channel and content. He's gotten a lot of new stuff. His giveaway and experience films have grown in size and cost. Today, he's investing millions of dollars every month on his content, but that's only because he's making more money.

He's always made it a point to put a significant portion of his earnings into his content… The numbers have just become much larger.

5. MRBEAST SAYS: THUMBNAILS ARE IMPORTANT

What people see before clicking to watch a video is critical. It is time well spent to develop an appealing still picture or thumbnail. Consider yourself a viewer; what would compel you to click or tap?

Remember that your thumbnail will be drastically reduced on mobile . So make your copy large and hence brief. Make sure your stills and thumbnails are visually attractive and easy to grasp.

Try new things. Experiment with brightness and hue. Examine what works.

With TubeBuddy and Thumbnail Analyzer, you can A/B test thumbnails and profit from AI learning (disclosure: TubeBuddy is a BENlabs item).

6. SET AND EXCEED EXPECTATIONS, SAYS MRBEAST
Hook viewers right away and don't let up.

A fantastic video title and thumbnail capture attention, but you must follow through on whatever promises you make. Consider your image and description to be expectations setters.

Your material should continually exceed or at the very least meet—the standards you establish. If not, you're clickbaiting, which no one enjoys.

7. MRBEAST SAYS: AUDIENCE OUTPERFORMS ALGORITHM
Algorithms are a strange and hazy idea. You can't satisfy The Algorithm (The Algorithm is excellent. But you can delight an audience (all praise The Algorithm). Particularly when the audience includes folks like you.

"Anytime you say the word algorithm, just replace it with audience," Mr. Beast advises. "Did the algorithm dislike that video?" No. That video was disliked by the audience."

All content algorithms seek to do is match individuals with the information they want to view. You can save a lot of time and effort by thinking about people rather than algorithms.

Get them to click, then keep them intrigued, and The Algorithm will reward you.

8. MRBEAST SAYS:

MrBeast is MrBeast. We understand how profound this is. He identified his niche and pursued it. It required a lot of effort and a few mistakes. If you look back at his early stuff, you'll see that it's not that complex, but it's rather clever. Even as he expanded his content business and acquired a slew of fantastic gear, his general video style has remained consistent.

MrBeast cannot be replicated, but any content producer may study MrBeast's content development playbook and apply it to their own material. So go ahead and try it.

9. KONNICHIWA, HABLO DEUTSCHE? SAYS MRBEAST.

Given that we authored this in English, we'll presume English is your first language. If so, that's great. If not, please accept our apologies for what we're sure is a poor translation.

Consider catering to a larger audience as a content developer by providing material in many languages. YouTube will try its utmost to provide closed captions in other languages, but we all know how unpredictable AI-generated subtitles can be.

If you have a popular video, try translating it into other languages to reach previously untapped consumers. The Procedure The audience will recognize your efforts.

MrBeast cannot be replicated, but any content producer may study MrBeast's content development playbook and apply it to their own material. So go ahead and try it.

10. CTR + RETENTION = WIN, SAYS MRBEAST.

The essential metrics that any content producer should monitor are click-through rate (CTR - how many people noticed your item and opted to click or tap) and audience retention (how many of those individuals hung around to watch). CTR measures how appealing your title and thumbnail are.

Audience retention reflects the quality of your material.

When it comes down to it, these two indicators are what define a content creator's success on a specific platform. Consider all facts, but avoid being paralyzed by analytical paralysis. You're doing it well if your CTR and retention rates are high.

11. MRBEAST SAYS: LEARN FROM YOUR ERRORS.

Mistakes are unavoidable, but they become failures only when we fail to learn from them. Someone famous from history probably articulated it better. The point is still valid.

Every possible lesson from each video should be extracted. If you've got a hit on your hands, wonderful; keep doing it. Consider all of the elements above when determining why a video hardly made a difference. Determine where people are leaving and ask yourself why. Then resolve the issue.

MrBeast's advise to budding makers is simple: try things, learn, and repeat.

12. BENLABS SAYS: WE ARE HERE TO ASSIST.

Content success needs originality, persistence, and a slew of other wonderful attributes. Remember what is important to you. Learn from your accomplishments and failures. Consider audiences before algorithms, but most importantly, strive. And keep us in mind when you become famous.

WHERE DO CREATIVES GET PAID?

Remove the uncertainty from influencer agreements. The BENlabs AI matching tool examines your content and audience before recommending your profile to marketers seeking for the ideal contributors to promote their goods and stories.

Printed in Great Britain
by Amazon